EVERYDAY FLOWERS

EVERYDAY FLOWERS

Growing, Arranging, and Living with Your Flowers

Photographs by Beth Maynor

Text and Arrangements by Norman Kent Johnson

LONGSTREET PRESS
Atlanta, Georgia

Published by
LONGSTREET PRESS, INC.
2150 Newmarket Parkway
Suite 102
Marietta, Georgia 30067

Printed in Singapore
94 93 92 91 90   5 4 3 2 1

Library of Congress Catalog Card Number: 90-60750

ISBN 0-929264-39-8

This book was printed by Tien Wah Press in Singapore.
The text type was set in Caslon by Typo-Repro
Service, Inc., Atlanta, Georgia. Design by Laura Ellis.

For
Spence and Bill
my children
whose spirits of love and discovery
and celebration of life
are the source of
one of my greatest joys
— B. M.

For
Bertie and Earnest
who planted the garden of my innocence
Meredith
who planted the seeds of truth
Helen
whose garden of the earth
is second only to
the garden of her heart
— N. K. J.

CONTENTS

ACKNOWLEDGMENTS

Everyday Flowers would not have been possible
without the help of our gardening friends.
We thank them for their patience and encouragement.
Most of all, we thank them for their flowers, their gardens
and their homes, which were our "studio."

In Birmingham: Betsy Brown; Alleen Cater;
Leslie Chastain; Chris Childs; Mary Catherine Crowe;
Peggy Dobbs; Marjorie Johnston; Bob and Rebecca Moody;
Philip Morris; Mary Margaret Todd; Toni Tully;
Louise Wrinkle; Billy Angel, The Garden Shop;
Carol Barton, Barton's Nursery.

In Atlanta: Becky Baxter, Eve Davis,
Dan B. Franklin, Ryan Gainy, Ray Simmons.

In Courtland, Alabama: Martha Ann Gilchrist.

In Millbrook, Alabama: Isabel Hill.

In Hillsboro, Alabama: Joye Bailey, David Woodall.

And special thanks to:
Candice Connard, for believing in us early on;
Michael Habrat, for being sage, saint and right-hand man.

Garden photos were taken in the gardens of
Becky Baxter, Eve Davis, Dan B. Franklin,
Martha Ann Gilchrist, Beth Maynor
and the Iris Garden in the Birmingham Botanical Garden.

INTRODUCTION

Everyday Flowers started with a simple proposition: Let's make one arrangement, once a week, for one full year. And let's use only garden flowers—things that we could grow ourselves.

This idea grew not because we're florists (we are not) but because we love gardening. And like most gardeners, we feel a missionary urge to share this love. Growing and arranging flowers give us so much pleasure, we feel obliged to make a convert any way we can. And we believe the best way to accomplish a conversion is to be simply, completely honest.

When we first began this project, we assumed that it would take a year. It's taken two. It's taken longer partly because we started out in winter. Although our gardens had been planned for interest through the year, we really hadn't planted them for heavy-duty cutting. Also, the fact that we needed something new and different each week meant that we had to grow a much expanded range of plants. And plants take time to grow. We did make use of our existing plants and some fast-growing annuals that first year, but we couldn't take advantage of the bulbs, perennials and shrubs we planted because they weren't sufficiently established.

We also needed the second year to fix the problems of the first. Most of the arrangements that we made that first year were mixed bouquets. According to that formula of "even distribution," each type of flower was inserted, stem by stem, into a block of florist foam. Flowers were mingled all together in a rather artful way that scattered colors, shapes and sizes throughout the vase. Pleasant, but predictable, and wholly artificial. We were in big trouble, even though we didn't really know it at the time.

Sometime towards the end of the first year, however, something wonderful happened. We walked into a friend's house where we'd planned to work that day, set down our pails of flowers that were soon to be arranged and started gathering containers. When we came back to those pails, we almost dropped a vase. Those bunched-up flowers looked terrific. They looked like exactly what they were — a garden gathering. Suddenly we realized a bit of truth: we had been *dis*arranging.

Flowers in the garden do not grow in mixed bouquets; they grow in clumps and bunches. Even if they're planted close together, every plant remains distinct. We see it as a single mass of foliage, stems and blooms. Unwittingly, we had been cutting gardening vignettes. We had been gathering a bunch of stems from one type plant, stuffing it in our gathering pail and then repeating that procedure with its neighbors until the pail was full. Although we hadn't thought "arrangement," that's what we had instinctively collected.

Arranging is not, then, a thing we do to flowers in a vase. It's something that we do with flowers in the garden. Every planted combination is a growing arrangement. It is the result of horticulture bordering on art. Plants are placed together because they all have similar needs and also because the gardener likes the way they look combined. Such natural bouquets filled ·our gardens. And we had been throwing it all away whenever we "arranged."

Since that day, we've tried to make arrangements that make sense. Garden sense. Most flower combinations come directly from the garden. If flowers do not share a bed, they rarely share a vase.

Sometimes, of course, we have mixed flowers that weren't companions in the garden. But almost always,

ASTILBE (*Astilbe x rosea* Peach Blossom) (*Astilbe x arendsii* Avalanche) CAROLINA PHLOX (*Phlox carolina* Miss Lingard)

Dependable perennials are mainstays of the garden and of this simple yet long-lasting arrangement. The spikey stems of Peach Blossom and Avalanche astilbe mingle pleasantly with the more open clusters of Miss Lingard phlox. The astilbe's fern-like foliage adds depth and weight to the base of the flowers in this arrangement from a High Spring garden.

these will have some natural connection or relationship. They may, for example, have a similar shape or color, or identical branching habits. Other times, however, they may be a combination that does not exist in the garden but could. And on occasions we have mixed flowers just because they seem to fit together. They were in bloom at the same time, and that was logic enough.

Our goal has been to celebrate each flower as we find it, not as we would have it be. Nothing is wired or glued or changed in any way. And with few exceptions, we have used no florist foam or other mechanics. We simply stuff until the vase is full. And if a flower arches, twists or stands straight up in the garden, it arches twists or stands straight up in the vase. If it grows in bunches, we've used a bunch. If it doesn't bloom profusely, we've used it sparingly. And if it's not in bloom at all? Foliage, stems and seedheads are a natural occurrence in the garden, so we've let them be a part of our arranging.

To many people, these arrangements don't look "everyday." They are not just a few stems dropped in a vase. Most of them are big, and some are downright ostentatious. But that's the point. When a garden is flower-filled, with more on the way, you can afford the luxury of making big arrangements. The day may come when flowers will be scarce, but in the meantime, give in to abundance. No matter what you've heard, the Modernists are wrong. "Less is more" is just an excuse for making do with not enough. More is more, and too much is just fine.

Other people may complain that many of these arrangements do not look arranged. They're not, not at least according to the typical definitions. They're just a bunch of flowers in a vase. If nothing else, we hope to make the process of arranging flowers so completely simple and nonthreatening that people who have never done it will give it a try. That's the missionary zeal. If we can successfully convert one nonarranging gardener to this delightful world of flowers, we will be happy.

In addition to presenting the arrangements found in our gardens, *Everyday Flowers* shows us in the garden year-round, through six seasons of growth, cutting flowers, branches, leaves—whatever was offered—to bring indoors. We have recorded the ways we value a garden, the ways we live with flowers in our homes and the things we have learned about gathering flowers and displaying them for the greatest pleasure. All is in celebration of nature's cycle that brings the freshness of early blooms and the drama of bare branches in a winter garden, the soft pastels of a springtime garden and the intensity of autumn's orange, flowers found along the roadside that can join garden flowers in a vase. It is a simple invitation to enjoy fresh flowers, every day.

FLOWERS IN THE GARDEN

n the beginning, there was a garden; it was the best place in the world. It had every kind of flower that there was, and they bloomed all the time. You could pick them if you wanted to because nobody ever said you couldn't. You could build a secret clubhouse underneath the cedar tree and roads between the roses. You could play Tarzan on wisteria, loves-me/loves-me-not with daisies and pirates in the lily pond. The only thing you couldn't do, except in an emergency, was use the bathroom in the bushes.

Why were we allowed to perpetrate these travesties—guileless though they may have been? Because the gardener was someone whom we loved, and who loved us more. Parent, grandparent, aunt, uncle, neighbor or good family friend—someone somewhere planted that first garden of our heart.

Today, we've grown beyond that garden of our innocence. We no longer play at pirates, nor do we make fairy rings of straw or autumn leaves. We weed out the dandelions, and we don't grow roses because we heard that they take lots of work. We've grown in age and stature, but maybe we haven't grown enough in wisdom. We've given up naiveté, and we've forgotten how to dream. Most of us have also lost that magic gardener who loved us so completely.

Yes, we are all grown up today, and so is our
garden. It is carefully designed in some new-fashioned
style that doesn't have much use for flowers. Perhaps
there are some daffodils and daylilies, but mostly we
have trees and shrubs and lawn. We do have a terrace,
which is furnished like a living room (and used about
as much as that room in the house). It also has a
fountain and some pots of annuals—all one type, of
course—that give us color from late spring until frost.
On the whole, it's quite attractive, but it's not a garden.
It's just a lot we paid to have landscaped.

And yet, we can hear little voices squealing with delight, calling the beloved name we used to call that long-lost gardener. "May we play pirates, please?" And it is we who answer back, "Yes, but don't fall in."

The joys and fantasies of childhood are as innocent today as when we were children. And to a child who doesn't know old-fashioned from new, a landscape is a garden. They're not aware that something's missing. Because they've never seen a foxglove in bloom, they've never known that its flowers fit their fingers. They've never sipped a honeysuckle. They've never known a garden. They only know this place. And it is what they'll think of, someday, when they're missing us.

We could justify this book if only for the children, who deserve the magic we have known. They have a right to flowers and to gardens. Considering the problems they will likely face someday, they may need them even more than we.

We must give them what they need because we need it too. Somewhere deep inside us, there's a very personal longing—awkward to explain but there—to be a child again. We need to find our way back to that garden of our youth—that place where life was simple, yet enchanted.

That garden is right outside the door. It's jam-packed full of flowers—daffydils and snappydragons, hollyhocks, and Marjorie golds. It's covered up with columbine, completely rampant with roses and head-high in goldenrod, phlox, black-eyed Susans, plume poppy, sunflowers and zinnias. Can't you see them? Close your eyes.

A garden starts with dreams, and no matter what you've heard, dreaming the dream is the hardest part of all for us grownups. It's tough to admit that we want something totally impractical, completely non-adult.

Remember, however, that no one has to know that you are doing this. Not yet. Daydreams live in the privacy of the mind. So muster your courage and get to work.

Fantasies need fuel to sustain them; in this case, that means we need some basic information. We need to see with clarity and specificity the garden of our dreams. We need to see it filled with flowers, and we need to know those flowers' names.

Reference books, gardening magazines and catalogs can help. But nothing is so telling as to see those flowers one-on-one. Botanical gardens, public parks, historic gardens and the gardens of your friends are places to start putting names to faces. Be sure to take along a notebook and a camera and start a filing system, however simple. A cardboard box, ring binder or photo album will do just fine. The important thing is to keep the information you've collected and to keep it growing. Whether we are amateurs or seasoned veterans, learning plants is something we shall do forever.

There does, however, come a time when we stop making lists and start to plant. But first, we need a place.

Since a cutting garden is intended as a place to grow, and not for show, it is sheer bliss for the beginning gardener. It can be located out of sight—a plus for the nervous and uncertain—and it doesn't take a vast amount of time, effort or expense to get it started. All you need is a sunny spot behind the garage, along a drive or alleyway, or some other out-of-the-way location, a convenient source of water and a little rototilling to break up the soil. Incorporating sand and compost also helps.

At its simplest, a cutting garden can be made of nothing but annuals from seed. In a month, and sometimes less, it goes from bare ground to abundance.

Seeds are cheap and easy to grow, and you get buckets of blooms from every pack. And when those flowers start to fade or fail to meet your expectations, you can rip them out and put in something else.

Because it is a place of quick rewards, a cutting garden of annuals is perfect for the inexperienced gardener. Instead of waiting months or years for trees, shrubs and perennials to reach maturity, you can watch an annual get taller every day. And then it blooms. And then it's done. The confidence and satisfaction that annuals bring, however, stay with us forever.

As we grow in skill and confidence, the day will come when we can step beyond the cutting garden's safety and make the garden of our dreams reality.

The flower garden is that place. We've pictured it each time we've heard that magical word "garden." We've seen the roses climbing through the railings of the fence, the hollyhocks beside the wall and the sundial at the center of the herb knot. We also know those shady, secret spots beneath the mock orange and weigela, and the arbor garlanded with clematis, wisteria, honeysuckle and jasmine. It is the garden of our heart's desire.

The flower garden is filled with every type of blooming plant that we can grow; it uses them in every conceivable way. Some of these plants will take the form of floral architecture: crisp-clipped hedges, topiary, espaliered and pollarded trees, allees and geometrical parterres. Plants in island beds, mixed borders, shrubbery screens and mingled hedges, broadleaf evergreens and ornamental trees also shape the garden's spaces but in softer, naturalistic ways. And lofty shade trees rise to form the garden's ceiling.

Tiny plants and bulbs find happy homes beneath their larger-growing peers. They also fill the cracks in pavings, chink the joints in walls and spill into the

lawn. No surface is allowed to go unplanted. Columns, tree trunks, lamp and gateposts, fences and even the walls of the house are camouflaged with climbing and twining plants.

Although it is exuberant, the flower garden tends to be a rather tidy place. After all, this is the garden of a connoisseur. Each plant takes its place according to the way it grows and for the role it plays. And every plant is tended with affection. Each plant in the garden is a personal acquaintance of the gardener; tending to its needs is simply part of being friends.

Each of us will make the garden of our heart's desire in different ways. Its size, shape and character will be determined by our property, the climate and our personalities. But each of us can make a garden that is magical—a garden where the child in us can grow to full maturity and yet remain a child.

FLOWERS IN THE HOME

here are people in this world — otherwise normal and well-adjusted people — who freeze in terror when faced with a bunch of fresh cut flowers. 'I can't arrange these things,' they sigh desperately; 'I'm not artistic.' So they cram those flowers into something like a jelly jar and hide them in the kitchen, never realizing they've just made an arrangement.

We've forgotten what arranging is all about. It *can* be a work of art, but it doesn't *have* to be. The first — really the only — goal of making an arrangement is delight.

We make arrangements, not because they're elegant, even though they are, and not because it's trendy to do so, because it's not. We do it because it makes us happy. Flowers are pretty and meaningful; when we place them in a vase, *they* are the art.

Much like paintings, porcelains and pieces of sculpture, arrangements have a certain artistic value. Unlike pigments, clay or metal, however, the nature of a flower as the raw material of an arrangement isn't changed. We celebrate its unaffected and intrinsic beauty. And even though the composition may be artful, it isn't really 'art' not, at least, according to the definition we prefer: Time passes; art endures.

PREVIOUS PAGE: GOLDEN SUNBURST
LILIES (*Lilium Golden Sunburst*)
BONANZA DAYLILIES (*Hemerocallis*
Bonanza)
QUEEN ANNE'S LACE (*Daucus carota*)
LARKSPUR (*Delphinium exaltatum*)
PURPLE GLORY SALVIA (*Salvia x
superba* Purple Glory)

This basket on a sunny porch is filled with country garden treasures: Golden Sunburst lilies, Bonanza daylilies, larkspur, Purple Glory salvia and Queen Anne's lace. Although the heat of the English Summer day forces the lilies to open completely, they will reclose somewhat at night.

VICTORIA SALVIA (*Salvia farinacea* Victoria)
EUROPEANA ROSE (*Rose* Europeana)
WILD AGERATUM (*Eupatorium coelestinum*)
BRIGHT LIGHTS COSMOS (*Cosmos sulphureus* Bright Lights)
PORTOLA GIANT GAILLARDIA (*Gaillardia grandiflora* Portola Giant)

This tiny little vase is like a summer microcosm. Arranged in hand during an early morning inspection of the garden, the flowers were simply dropped into the little crystal vase as they were gathered. Quick, easy and totally endearing, this little nosegay still seems to sparkle with dew.

Flowers are transient. They're fresh for a few days, and then they fade. That quality is what makes flowers precious. They have meaning also because they remind us of our own mortality. Like flowers, our lives have seasons, and arranging flowers from the garden—flowers we have grown—adds to our understanding of life's cycles and our awareness of its continuity. We've planted the flowers and tended them. We've watched

CRIMSON MONARCH ZINNIAS (*Zinnia elegans* Crimson Monarch)
PURPLE PRINCE ZINNIAS (*Zinnia elegans* Purple Prince)
EXQUISITE ZINNIAS (*Zinnia elegans* Exquisite)
POLAR BEAR ZINNIAS (*Zinnia elegans* Polar Bear)
EUROPEANA ROSE (*Rosa* Europeana)
VIRGIN'S BOWER CLEMATIS (*Clematis virginiana*)
SNOW-ON-THE-MOUNTAIN (*Euphorbia bicolor*)
LIRIOPE (*Liriope muscari*)

This full and somewhat opulent Deep Summer arrangement counterpoints the richness and detail of its dramatic environment. Four types of zinnias were first set into place, along with a cluster of bright red Europeana roses. Next, virgin's bower clematis and the variegated foliage of snow-on-the-mountain were tucked into the edges. Finally, the spiky flowers of liriope were added as a topping accent.

them grow and change throughout the seasons. We have been partners with nature in the garden. And when we gather and arrange those flowers, we complete a cycle. We bring the joy and wonder of our relationship with nature into our homes.

Have you ever noticed in books and magazines that a pictured room will almost always have at least one vase of flowers? The fresh flowers are there because they bring a room to life. They add a spark of animation to an empty room; they say, "This is a home."

Arrangements of complementary colors
have an automatic sense of unity—
even when a rich diversity of flowers
are combined. This freewheeling mix
of Deep Summer blooms makes use of
spikey Apricot Brandy celosia, Red
Marietta and Sophia marigolds, the
button-like flowers of Hageana Aurea
globe amaranth, and sprigs of
Candlelight peppers. Tucked into this
fiery blend are spikes of orchid
Charming buddleia and rich magenta
Marine heliotrope.

Since flowers are important to the looks and feelings of a room, they should convey the appropriate look and feel. They should say, without the slightest doubt, "This is *my* home." If those flowers in that vase are flowers you have grown, every chance of strangeness is erased because garden flowers are completely personal. They're also fresher, less expensive, more convenient to obtain and much more varied than most types of flowers you can buy. Even the finest shops cannot supply the rich diversity afforded by your garden.

Garden flowers come in every color, shape and size; they bloom in every season. Not all at once, of course, but each one in its time. Consequently, they always look just right. There never is a need to ask, "Why tulips in December?" because our tulips bloom in spring. And in December we collect the treasures of that time.

Arranging garden flowers helps us see our gardens and our homes in new and reassuring ways. They strengthen the bond between our rooms inside the house and that most splendid room outdoors. We see the house within the garden; we also see the garden from the house, through doors and windows. And we can make that visual connection tangible. When we fill a vase with garden flowers, we bring the substance of our garden right into our home.

Arranging lets us see each flower as an individual. In the garden, we tend to see flowers in a group—a clutch of irises, a bunch of marigolds, hydrangeas as a shrub. But in the close-at-hand perspective of the vase, we can see each one in detail. We can study it and get to know it's singular attraction. No two flowers are alike. Even those from the same plant are slightly different. And close examination lets us see that quality within the garden as a whole.

When we study flowers in this way, we can let each one assume the spotlight. Even if a flower is not a major garden feature, we can let it play a featured role in an arrangement. The flowers of dill, for example, tend to be a yellow haze out in the garden. In a vase, however, their delicate starburst arrangement on the stem seems bold, their color more intense, and their beauty becomes apparent. Modest little flowers like witch hazel, American columbine, and miniature irises also get an ego boost when they become the celebrated flower. And once we've let them be a star indoors, we'll never overlook them in the garden.

When we let our gathering become attuned to subtlety, even small discoveries become dramatic. The way the pale October sun illuminates the fading foliage of American beech is easily overlooked. But once you've seen it, it will change forever your appreciation of that tree in autumn. And the bravery of a daffodil confronted by the sudden return of frost is poignant and inspiring. We gather just a single stem and take it to a vase because it's taken our heart.

Arranging teaches us about our gardens, its flowers, the seasons and nature. It also teaches us about ourselves. When we make our first arrangement, we know that it's not perfect. And yet, we also know that fact is unimportant. In time, we will become more practiced and more confident. But in the meantime, we're learning lessons much more meaningful than composition's regimen of art. We've learned to see a beauty that cannot fade. The artfulness of nature endures despite the passing of time.

TOP LEFT: SASSAFRAS (*Sassafras albidum*)
AMERICAN COLUMBINE (*Aquilegia canadensis*)
JAPANESE MAPLE FOLIAGE (*Acer palmatum*)
TRUMPET HONEYSUCKLE (*Lonicera sempervirens* sulphurea)

East meets west in both the setting and the materials of this exuberant High Spring display. The airy, fragrant blooms of native sassafras and the exotic, bell-like, orange-and-yellow flowers of American columbine are both well-suited to the character of the Oriental bowl. The delicate foliage of Japanese maple and the lobed leaves of honeysuckle continue the illusion of calligraphy. An old-fashioned metal frog, secured with floral adhesive, forms a necessary anchor for the woody branches.

Between the Garden and the Vase

**A**rranging builds relationships. Indeed, it forms a series of connections. Flower to flower, flowers to vase, arrangement to location—each of these relationships contributes to that unity that is arranging's goal.

Frequently this harmony is carefully controlled. Flowers are selected and arranged by formula. Location and container, the mix of flower colors, shapes and sizes and the placement of each flower are determined by the methods and mechanics of a style. Everything is predetermined; nothing is left to chance.

But something is left out if arrangements have no sense of spontaneity. At their best, they express their genesis—that spark of evolution that conveys a flower's origins. Arrangements should make manifest the bond between the garden and the vase.

The process of arranging usually starts indoors. We pick a location, choose a container, and then we make a list of flowers that we think will work. And then we take that list into the garden. But it ought to work the other way around. Arranging shouldn't be a thing we do *to* flowers in a vase. We do it *with* them, in the garden. When we plant, we make arrangements to have flowers all year long. We carefully consider plants by color, shape and size, and then we plant that combination.

When we let the garden be the source and inspiration for the flowers in our homes, we never have to question whether they will work. We can see they do. The only thing that we must do is harvest. We cut, responsively, because those flowers are in bloom. Instinctively, we cut a bunch of this, a bit of that, because those plants are close together. We gather up, inherently, a soupçon of the garden.

Although we have essentially created our arrangement, it is not complete until it takes its place inside. That's our final goal. Before we reach that point, however, several things must happen, step by step, along the path that forms the link between the garden and the vase.

Gathering is one of the great joys of gardening. It is the harvesting of dreams. We've invested a lot of time and love in planting and tending our flowers with care and expectation; now, those promises have been fulfilled. The flowers in our garden can be as fragile as our dreams, however, so we need to handle them with care. When we gather, we must safeguard beauty, freshness and longevity.

Water is essential to a flower. Indeed, it forms the greater portion of a flower's structure. Deep inside a stem, bundles of little tubes called xylem and phloem provide a flower's "plumbing" and its skeleton. These tubes are filled with water, which keeps them rigid and the flower head erect.

When we cut a flower, we separate it from its source of water—its roots and the earth's reservoir of moisture. We must, therefore, provide an alternate supply. And we must take it with us when we gather. As soon as a stem is cut, it should be just as quickly placed into a pail of water. Haste really is important. After a stem is cut, it begins to seal that wound almost immediately, much as our own bodies seal a cut. This scaling is a natural defense which helps conserve each molecule of water in the stem. Even so, a flower will continue to lose moisture through its leaves and petals to evaporation. So it is important to take water to the

PASSIONALE DAFFODIL
(*Narcissus* Passionale)
FLORIDA LEUCOTHOE
(*Leucothoe populifolia*)
COMMON BOX (*Buxus sempervirens*)
ITALIAN ARUM (*Arum italicum*)

The rich green foliages of leucothoe, box and arum help give fullness to this airy composition of pink-trumpet daffodils from an Antecedent Spring garden. The box was simply "stuffed" into the antique celery glass, with no pretensions of grace. That's provided by the arching stems of leucothoe and the marbled leaves of arum. Finally, the daffodils were set into the armature of greenery.

plant, and not the other way around.

When you gather, use a clean, quick cut to minimize the damage to the stem. Although some arrangers say that you should use a knife because it doesn't crush the stem, most people find that scissor-action shears let them cut faster. And that's what's really important. Use whichever method is most efficient. Just be sure to use a sharp, clean tool and take the cut diagonally, just above a leaf node. This exposes the maximum amount of surface through which the flower can drink.

If you gather away from home, you may not be able to take a pail of water with you. You can, however, take along some plastic garbage bags. After cutting, place the flowers in the bag head-down and close the end. If possible, enclose the entire flower, stem and all. It also helps to place a damp sponge in the bottom of the bag to help increase humidity around the flower heads. A blunt rather than diagonal cut is also recommended for field gathering.

Once flowers have been gathered, they need to be "conditioned" with a long, deep soak in water. For maximum efficiency, conditioning is best done in a cool, dark, humid place like a basement. Remove each flower, one at a time, from the collecting pail and place it in a tall, clean container of lukewarm water. Along the way, strip off excess foliage and remove about an inch of stem, using once again a clean, diagonal cut. Stand each flower neck deep (or as deep as possible) in order to let every available bit of stem have access to the water.

If you've gathered flowers away from home, a two-step process of conditioning is recommended. Place the flowers in a lukewarm pail, as above, and let them soak for a half-hour. Then transfer them to a fresh pail of lukewarm water, again recutting one-half inch of stem along the way. Even with this extra care, chances are some flowers will have wilted. Sometimes these can be revived by totally submerging them in a cool bath overnight.

Woody stems and branches need a different kind of treatment. Using a sharp knife, scrape away about two inches of bark from the cut end of the stem before it's placed in water. If flowers or foliage is wilted, crush the ends of the stems with a hammer before inserting them into the water. You may also try using warm (baby-bath temperature) water to accelerate absorption.

The best time to collect is early morning, when the air is moist and cool, or just before dark when flowers have revived from midday heat. It also helps to water plants the day before you gather so that they will be at their maximum freshness. Typically, morning-gathered flowers can get by with a few hours of conditioning before they're placed in an arrangement. Flowers gathered in the evening, on the other hand, can enjoy the benefit of overnight conditioning; on the whole, they tend to last a little longer than morning-gathered blooms.

After flowers have had their soak, they're ready to arrange. Just be sure to recut every stem before it goes into the vase. A tablespoon of household bleach to every quart of water may be used to help inhibit the growth of bacteria. No matter what you've heard, however, never use anything but bleach. The stuff that is supposed to feed the flowers also feeds algae.

CONTAINERS

Anything that's large enough to hold a bunch of stems and some water can be a container for arranging. And yet, a container is much more than a receptacle; it's half of the arrangement. Consequently, we should give some thought to what makes a desirable companion for our flowers.

Surprisingly, only two things are required of a good container. First, it must be pretty, even when it's empty. Like any good accessory, a container ought to suit the mood and character of a room. Whether it's an official vase or something else that's waterproof and hollow, the container that works best is an everyday appointment to a room—worthy of a second look, but not gaudy or bizarre.

The second requirement of a good container is its shape. A chunky cylinder, slightly taller than its width, is the nearly perfect shape for flowers. The straight sides can help hold flower stems erect, or flowers can be set at an angle to create a network for supporting other stems. Short, tall and in-between, cylindrical containers lend themselves to almost every type of flower and situation. Aside from that contemporary classic the

NEVADA ROSE (*Rosa* Nevada)
SPRING BEAUTY SWEET WILLIAM (*Dianthus barbatus* Spring Beauty Mix)
MAXISTAR COLUMBINE (*Aquilegia longissima* Maxistar)
FREEDOM HEUCHERA (*Heuchera sanguinea* Freedom)
WORMWOOD (*Artemisia absinthium*)

Gentle harmonies of High Spring color reverberate throughout this small writing table landscape. The brilliant yellow stamens of Nevada roses are repeated in the exotically shaped blooms of Maxistar columbine. The mingled pink and white of Spring Beauty sweet William is echoed in both the berry-like flowers of Freedom heuchera and the flowers on the vase. And a single stem of wormwood foliage picks up the grey of the painted walls.

clear glass cylinder, wines carafes, iced tea and water pitchers and various types of crocks and churns are basically cylindrical in shape. So, too, are most drinking glasses, storage jars and even storage tins.

Flared vases offer a useful variation on the cylinder shape. They immediately set the stems of flowers at an angle. And since the mouth is wider than the base, flowers can spread out in a graceful, upright way. Be wary of exaggerated, trumpet-shaped containers. Although they can be very elegant, they tend to get top-heavy. Even if sufficiently heavy to be steady, these containers can easily look out of balance when they're filled with flowers.

Wide, shallow containers such as bowls and soup tureens are tough to use effectively. Their smooth, rounded sides and bottoms give no place for stems to rest. Their width also makes it difficult to fill out the center of an arrangement. These containers typically demand some sort of mechanic—florist foam, frogs or pinholders. Or they can be packed with dense, short-stemmed flowers or leafy branches to form an armature for upright stems. Their elegance of shape, however, makes these containers worth the extra trouble they create.

The finish and materials of containers also deserve a bit of attention. Containers with plain finishes will tend to lend themselves to a greater variety of flowers and locations. Similarly, the more ornate the surface decoration, the less flexible the container.

Since containers are the only permanent part of an arrangement, they need to be quite durable so that they can be used again and again. Metal, heavy pottery and porcelain are ideal materials for containers. Clear or opaque glass is also a popular material for vases; if it's not too fragile, glass can be an attractive and versatile material.

DIXIE IRIS (*Iris hexagona*)
MOUNTAIN BLUET (*Centaurea montana*)
GARDEN SAGE (*Salvia officinalis*)

The pale lavender of Dixie iris flowers are carried at the ends of gently arching stems. The elegance of their line and color are reinforced by upright stems of garden sage flowers and the starburst blooms of mountain bluet. The openness of all these High Spring flowers lends itself to a simple, unassuming placement and container.

But when you work with clear glass, you double your trouble. You can see everything; sometimes, you can see too much—like a jumble of stems and murky water. Certain flowers, however, like springtime bulbs and flowering branches that have interesting stems, lend themselves quite easily to clear glass vases.

LOCATION

When choosing a place for fresh flowers in a room, it is important to think about the way those flowers will be seen. At eye level or elevated, against a background or in the center of a room, under a lamp or in natural sunlight—different places have different effects.

Flowers tend to look their best seen straight on, at or just below eye level. In dining rooms, living rooms or other sitting places, eye level is about forty inches above the floor. If we place our flowers at this height, we can look directly in their faces. Elevated spots such as mantlepieces, pedestals and bookcases can also be good locations, however. Even though they tend to place flowers overhead, they present them in full view. Such locations also keep flowers out of reach of busy little hands and, if you have them, cats.

Backgrounds directly affect the way we see our flowers. The planes and surfaces behind arrangements are as much a part of the composition as flowers and containers. When we place flowers near a wall, screen, bookcase or a massive piece of furniture, that vertical surface stops our view. And that creates a silhouette effect around the arrangement. We can see clearly the shapes and outline of the overall arrangement. But if we place our flowers at the center of a room, there is no solid background to set off the profile. Instead, the flowers are surrounded by light, air and space. The

result is a soft and airy quality, but the flowers also will look a little out of focus.

The color, pattern and texture of a background directly affect the color, texture and pattern of arrangements. Color, however, while it is one of the most exciting attributes of flowers, is really the least important consideration in selecting a location. Color is purely personal. If you like red roses in a room that is shocking pink, arrange red roses, by all means. There are no real rules for mixing hues. On the other hand, value will make a difference; the relative degree of light and dark in background colors will determine the reflectivity of a background. Keep in mind that the darker the background, the less reflection there will be and the crisper the appearance of the flowers. The texture and pattern of a background is essentially a matter of complexity. Busy backgrounds such as rough stone or brick walls, patterned papers or printed fabrics call for large and simple flowers. Small, frilly flowers will be nothing but a blur. Stark, simple surfaces, however, need richness and diversity of flower shapes and sizes as a contrast to the background's uniformity.

Lighting is by far the most important factor to consider in the selection of a location. Too often we ignore the drama lighting lends to flowers. Place a small arrangement under a lamp, and its presence fills a room. A well-aimed spotlight or an uplight on the floor intensifies colors and creates exciting plays of shadow within an arrangement. Natural sunlight works pure magic. The butter yellow of morning sun makes hot colors sizzle and soft colors seem luminescent. The golden orange of afternoon, on the other hand, makes flowers look electrified, glowing from within. Although it is not always possible to control the light that falls on an arrangement, if we can we ought to seize that opportunity and use it to our advantage.

Height, background and lighting all help us choose locations that increase our pleasure from arrangements. Another consideration should be the welfare of our flowers. We can extend an arrangement's life by placing it where it is free of drying drafts or direct, burning sunlight, and where it is out of reach.

Most flowers will keep longer if they are protected from drafts. The constant, low-humidity breeze of forced-air heat and cooling is deadly to flowers because it accelerates respiration. The flow of air across a flower speeds evaporation of water from the stems and petals, the dry air acting like a sponge that can draw a vast amount of water from a flower. While regular refilling of containers with cool water helps replenish moisture in the tissue of a flower, a periodic misting will create a beneficial microclimate within the center of arrangements. Cool temperatures also help maintain humidity.

Direct, intense sunlight can actually burn the delicate tissues of a flower. Water droplets on the surface of a petal act like lenses that focus and intensify sunlight into a burning, laser-like beam. And bright light bleaches the color from a flower as it bleaches fabrics.

Flowers need protection from physical damage as well as from drafts and direct sunlight. Brushing against a flower can bruise its petals and remove surface moisture. Unnecessary handling can also crimp or crush a stem and inhibit a flower's ability to drink. This danger is increased, of course, when arrangements are within the reach of household pets. Dogs and cats both have a taste for flowers and think they are great toys. Cats are especially fond of pulling arrangements apart and scattering the flowers through the house.

MECHANICS

The use of "gadgets" such as marbles and frogs rarely
makes arranging better; it merely gives us more control.
And that is not our goal. We prefer to let each flower
express its natural shape and character, so if we've
chosen our flowers and containers with care, the only
other things we really need are water and a little time.
If they help you make a start, however, use mechanics
to the best advantage of your flowers.

Glass marbles can be a definite help when
arranging flowers for loose, airy effects. They hold the
stem in place without affecting their angles or
direction. Marbles also let you fluff or reposition
flowers as you work because they do not grasp the
stems. Something to keep in mind is that since they
are smooth, glass marbles tend to move around as each
new stem is inserted. And that means that previously-
placed flowers move as well. This lack of control,
however, is the greatest virtue of glass marbles. Because
they prevent being too precise, they help avoid an
artificial stiffness.

Old-fashioned frogs — openwork cages of welded or
cast metal — can be useful tools, especially when
working with shallow or wide-mouthed containers. The
first few flower stems can be inserted into the grid to
establish an interlocking network or armature which
holds other stems in place. Frogs can also help hold
stems erect when using only a few flowers. The
problem, of course, is that when you look into the
container, you're likely to see the frog.

Glass frogs can be used in much the same fashion
as metal frogs. These cast-glass disks have several
holes, usually arranged in concentric circles, into which
stems are inserted. Their problem is that they only

hold stems vertically, which can result in flowers looking like flags. Used carefully, however, they can, like metal frogs, provide a secure, first-step framework for larger armatures of stems.

Unlike marbles, frogs and a few other mechanics, pinholders are nothing but a pain. They almost always make flowers look like they are standing at attention. Most are neither large enough nor heavy enough to support more than a few flowers. They have to be secured to the container with clay or floral adhesive. For any number of good reasons, try to avoid them altogether.

Florist foam is a very popular aid to arranging because it holds both water and flowers. Rather like a sponge, the foam can absorb a vast amount of water and hold it like a reservoir for use by the flowers it supports. It also allows inserting flowers at any angle. And that's the problem with florist foam: it allows too much control. By placing foam so that it stands above the rim of a container, for example, flowers can be placed so that they hang upside down. That position is fine for flowers that naturally arch, weep or trail, but flowers that normally grow upright have a decidedly unnatural appearance hanging head down. If the flowers are placed with regard for their natural shapes and characters, however, florist foam can be a useful tool, especially when working with a wide, shallow container like a bowl. Remember to carefully conceal the foam with flowers or foliage so that it can't be seen.

Chicken wire has been a mainstay for arrangers for generations. It offers an instant armature with openings sufficiently wide to accept large branches. Although chicken wire is frequently crumpled into a ball and stuffed into a vase, doing so tends to crush the wire mesh and complicate the process of inserting larger stems. A better technique is to use a sheet of wire

SUMMER SUN HELIOPSIS (*Heliopsis scabra* Summer Sun)
PICCOLO SUNFLOWERS (*Helianthus annuus* Piccolo)
ITALIAN WHITE SUNFLOWERS (*Helianthus annuus* Italian White)
BORDER BEAUTY ZINNIAS (*Zinnia elegans* Border Beauty)

A full-round arrangement of daisy-like flowers make a happy complement to the furnishings and appointments of a country-formal dining room. Since it can be viewed from every side, the arrangement was constructed from the top down to give fullness from all directions. Stems of Summer Sun heliopsis form the central mass of the composition; Piccolo and Italian White sunflowers and orange-to-red Border Beauty zinnias were then tucked in at random. These Deep Summer flowers are held in place with a metal florist frog.

across the top of a container. The wire can be held in place by crimping its tag-ends around the mouth of the container or by securing it with heavy-gauge, waterproof florist tape. Place an X of tape across the top of the wire and attach the ends to both sides of the container. For extra security, wrap the container's rim with several layers of tape to secure the edges of the wire.

There are many ways of "doing" flowers. We can simply drop a bunch of stems into a vase, or we can place them one by one. We may arrange according to the methods of a style, or we may break the rules and find a style that's all our own. The way that works the best for you is how it should be done.

Like gardening, arranging is a hands-on kind of thing. The only way we ever learn to do it is to do it. At first it seems completely awkward and unnatural, but if we are persistent — if we really want to learn — the skills and understanding will evolve.

As gardeners, that evolution starts the day we plant. We watch our flowers change from seedlings to maturity, and by the time they are in bloom, we know them intimately. We know exactly how they grow; we understand their attributes and personalities.

This knowledge is a great advantage when we gather flowers for arrangements. If we've planned and planted with care, the flowers in our garden have a natural affinity and rightness. The plants that bloom together go together, inherently. So all we have to do is cut.

When it comes to placing flowers into a container, the only rule we must observe is character of growth. We must let the shape and character of every flower tell us where it ought to go. We must let the flowers take control. We must respond to them with spontaneity and intuition.

Most of the arrangements in this book were made with what we call the clump-and-fluff technique. Place a bunch of one type flower into the container all at once, and let them fall against one side. Then place another bunch of shorter flowers against the opposite

MOON RIVER PEONY (*Paeonia* Moon River)
HELEN ALLWOOD PINKS (*Dianthus x allwoodii* Helen)
SPRING BEAUTY ALLWOOD PINKS (*Dianthus x allwoodii* Spring Beauty)
ROSE VERBENA (*Verbena canadensis*)
BONICA ROSE (*Rosa* Bonica)
LAMB'S EARS (*Stachys lanata*)
BRONZE FENNEL (*Foeniculum vulgare* Baloquese)
RUE (*Ruta graveolens*)

Sometimes the desire to cram flowers into a vase is irresistible. This densely-packed, yet delicate, array of High Spring blooms includes one pale pink Moon River peony, equally pastel Bonica roses and the deeper-toned Helen and Spring Beauty Allwood pinks. The vivid, glowing pink-colored flower is rose verbena. Completing the airy abundance are yellow blooms of rue, velvety gray lamb's ears and the frilly, fragrant foliage of bronze fennel.

side of the container. Finally, set a bunch of even shorter flowers in the center. Gently lift the whole arrangement a few inches, and let the flowers drop back into place. The result is pleasant, loose and asymmetrical. It also looks completely unaffected. It doesn't seem controlled because it's not.

Another method, used in some of our arrangements, is to insert each stem separately. Lay the first few stems at a diagonal across the rim of the container to create a series of Xs. This armature of stems becomes a framework that helps hold additional stems in place. As the quantity of flower stems increases, this armature becomes more intricate and more secure, so the last few flowers can be positioned exactly where desired.

As an arrangement evolves, it is sometimes necessary to remove or reposition a branch or stem. This is best done by clipping off the stem that must be moved with pruning shears. Don't try to pull the flower out of the container; you would quite likely move a lot of other things as well. If more than one stem doesn't seem quite right, however, it's better to take all the flowers out and start again. Don't take it to heart; just take them out. Mistakes are bound to happen.

How do you know when an arrangement is finished? If the vase won't hold another stem, chances are you're through. Like Vita Sackville-West, we like abundance; the best way to obtain it is to "cram, cram, cram" until the vase is filled to overflowing.

The other way to know when an arrangement's done is to run out of flowers. The best arrangement is the one that grows until there is no more to go in it. We simply can't dispute the Red Queen's logical advice to little Alice: "Start at the beginning, go on to the end, then stop."

ANTECEDENT
SPRING

 here comes a day when winter's grip relaxes, just a bit. A few days of bright sunshine and a little extra warmth is all it takes to rouse the garden out of slumber. The changes are subtle, to be sure, but something's happening. There's a faint but steady vibration deep within the earth. The bulbs are waking and buds are swelling. It is Antecedent Spring.

Almost overnight, the elm trees and red maples start to show a little touch of color in their buds. The tight-shut buds of daffodils begin to open, and one or two precocious ones explode into full bloom. The Lenten roses lift waxy heads above their tattered foliage. The more predictable early flowers like snowdrops, cyclamen, camellias, alders, daphne, quince, Cornelian cherry and crocuses start to bloom with more determination. Pansies, however, tend to sulk a bit while forsythia shows itself like a flamboyant little early bird.

PUSSY WILLOW (*Salix discolor*)
CAROLINA YELLOW JESSAMINE
(*Gelsemium sempervirens*)

Branches almost always need a simple background. Here, the switch-like stems of pussy willow are effectively displayed against a neutral, grey-painted wall. The willow's linework also picks up the pattern of floor, window mullions and shadows. The wiry stems of jessamine spill out of the top of the vase and clamber through the willow. A few bright yellow flowers help emphasize the delicate dusty yellow of the willow blooms.

Although any flower is welcome at this season, yellow ones are somehow best. The brilliance of their color is like distilled sunlight. Just a touch of yellow among the browns and grey is enough to make us feel the energy of nature's reawakening.

As the garden begins to wake, it is time for us to rise also and get busy in the garden. There is in fact some need for haste on our part because the weeds have been awake for quite a while and are already starting to creep across the surface of the beds. Now is the time to hoist them out so that later we will not have to disturb other plants.

The chores of Antecedent Spring are not especially numerous, but they are important. There are several things like weeding that we can do early on to save ourselves a lot of effort later. We can, for example, give our gardens the equivalent of a morning cup of coffee in the form of a low-nitrogen fertilizer. The fertilizer will give a boost to roots, which continue to grow below the surface as long as the ground isn't frozen. If we feed them now, we can get several weeks' jump on the time of active foliage growth. Now too is the time to get the dormant sprays in place. And if the winter has been dry, be sure to water. Winter winds can dry out plants as fast as anything. Do hold off on major pruning, however, even though this seems to be a good time to do it. If you let things come into bloom and take the flowers, you can enjoy the best of what the plants have to offer and at the same time accomplish a necessary task.

Antecedent Spring has its dangers, too. Plants are threatened by frost heave, sun scald and freeze damage from the quick return of cold. Since one day can be warm but the next morning frigid, we'll likely have to do a lot of dashing back and forth with armloads of straw, plastic sheeting or light-weight burlap to shelter newly-sprung plants.

But we must also be willing to let what happens happen. It is the destiny of certain plants to suffer harsh reprisals for their brash enthusiasm. The frost will almost always nip the flowers of Oriental

magnolias. And the daphne that perfumed the garden for almost a week may be snuffed out overnight. And yet, it is presumptuous of us to fret over the loss of these flowers; as part of nature's cycle, it happens every year. We've enjoyed those few delightful days of bloom, and when the forecast promises a freeze, we can always go out and cut like crazy for the house and bring the Antecedent Spring indoors.

ALBA PLENA CAMELLIA
(*Camellia japonica* alba plena)
AMABILIS CAMELLIA
(*Camellia japonica* amabilis)
SNOWFLAKE (*Leucojum vernum*)
ALDER (*Alnus rugosa*)

The bell-like flowers of snowflakes, with their little dots of green, rise above three perfect white camellia blooms. The placement of the camellias is partly for balance and partly because these flowers have short stems. Pieces of their foliage give a background to the airy snowflakes; a few twigs of brown alder cones pick up the hues of the stoneware jar, antique shawl and well-scrubbed tabletop.

RED MAPLE (*Acer rubrum*)
LENTEN ROSE (*Helleborus orientalis*)
NANDINA (*Nandina domestica*)

This arrangement's harmonies of color, line and texture were borrowed directly from the woodland garden where the flowers were collected. The Lenten roses were a groundcover beneath the lofty branches of the maple. Brought down to the scale of a vase, the winged seeds of the maple hang like tassels above the open faces of the Lenten roses. Winter-bronzed foliage of nandina echoes, at a smaller scale, the Lenten rose's leaves, which were too frost burned to be usable.

ABOVE: CABBAGE (*Brassica oleracea*)

These exotic flowers were left over
from autumn's vegetable garden. The
blossoms of bolted cabbage, along with
several of its leaves, create a delightful
and surprisingly elegant effect when
brought indoors. Simply arranged in a
glass bubble, they elevate this humble
eatable to the realm of ornamental
horticulture.

RIGHT: YOSHINO CHERRY
(*Prunus yedoensis*)

Set into the alcove of a circular stair,
this arrangement of cherry blooms
subtly repeats the flowing curves and
verticles of the steps, banister and
railing. The clear glass cylinder
becomes almost invisible when filled
with water; the linework of the
branches stands out against the
background of the wall.

HIGH
SPRING

 nce the last frost date is past, the garden's pace of change accelerates from weeks to days to hours. Where there were buds in the morning, we find full blooms by afternoon. Suddenly we are surrounded, almost overwhelmed, by flowers. We've made it to High Spring.

The flowers of this season fill the garden top to bottom with exuberant displays of color. The ground is carpeted with bloom; overhead, trees create a mingled canopy of fresh green foliage, flowers and bright patches of blue sky. And in between, the garden is suffused with blooming shrubs. It's as if a party-colored cloud had settled on the garden. No wonder that it's called High Spring. It truly makes us giddy.

Color in the High Spring garden comes in a big way. Flowering trees like dogwood, crabapple, hawthorn and the many types of plums and peaches create a mass of flowers sometimes thirty feet in height. This is also the season of big shrubs — spiraeas, azaleas, viburnums, kerria, mock orange, mountain laurel, deutzia and lilac — that can all be completely camouflaged with bloom. Even smaller growing plants such as irises, peonies, columbines, foxglove, pinks, sweet William and the early roses make a lot of blooms, so many that we almost never pay attention to the flowers as individuals. Everything is just a mass of bloom. However, High Spring's flowers are too beautiful not to be enjoyed as more than just a pile of color. Arrangements of these flowers let us see each one close up, in detail.

RIGHT: REEVES SPIREA (*Spiraea cantoniensis*)
LADY BANKS ROSE (*Rosa banksiae*)
YELLOW TRUMPET HONEYSUCKLE
(*Lonicera sempervirens* sulphurea)

Many of spring's finest flowers are large-growing, deciduous shrubs and vines. Although a few small snippets of these plants can be collected for use indoors, nothing captures their beauty better than using them full-sized. Here, the arching stems of Lady Banks rose and Reeves spirea rise dramatically from the tall, narrow vase. Long tendrils of yellow honeysuckle also reach full-length from the container. The effect is highly stylized, but it does express the spirit of these fine, old-fashioned plants.

Arranging also helps us keep pace with springtime's rapid changes. It makes us more aware of what blooms when, and that awareness can help us better plan our garden. The real concern is not so much sequence, however, as it is the color combinations that result when the vagaries of weather completely upset the usual order. Some years everything is late; other years everything comes early and all at once. Because that can sometimes make for jarring combinations, the springtime garden is better planned so that no matter when things bloom they all blend together. For the most part, springtime flowers come in soft pastels, all of which do work together, but some springtime plants — tulips, poppies and azaleas in particular — come in bold and brassy colors that can upset the overall visual harmony of the garden. Bright, true reds and orange are especially tricky. These colors make us think of warmer weather for one thing, and their brilliance tends to steal attention from less powerful colors. If used at all, strong-colored flowers must be tempered with generous amounts of white and green or placed where they will not compete with other plants.

For gardeners as well as plants, High Spring is a very busy season in the garden. Early on, there is a need to check for winter damage, to remove thick layers of mulch from beds and borders and generally "spruce" things up. Beds that have been damaged by frost heave will need to be reworked or reset.

This is also the time to feed the foliage of early bulbs for next year's bloom and to apply a light, low-nitrogen fertilizer to almost everything except irises, which do best when they're hungry. Various types of sprays, especially those for aphids that feed on tender growth, should also be applied before plants are damaged.

QUEEN ANNE'S LACE (*Daucus carota*)
BUTTERFLY WEED (*Asclepias tuberosa*)
YARROW (*Achillea filipendulina* Coronation Gold)
COREOPSIS (*Coreopsis grandiflora* Sunray)
MALTESE-CROSS (*Lychnis chalcedonica*)

Masses of wildflowers and garden blooms make a happy marriage in this exuberant celebration of High Spring. Several stems of dense, dusty orange butterfly weed were first set into place to form a base for taller stems of Queen Anne's lace. The more vivid orange of Maltese-cross forms a central accent while evenly-distributed stems of Sunray coreopsis and Coronation Gold yarrow fill the mass with glowing yellow highlights.

Planting is another exciting High Spring ritual. This is a time to set out annuals for later-season bloom and trees and shrubs of almost every kind. Try to purchase plants as soon as possible to get the best selection. Everybody will have spring fever, so there's sure to be a lot of competition at the nursery or garden center. And don't forget about spring bulbs. Even though this isn't time to plant, it is the time to plan for next year's flowering, so while your memory is fresh, make a note of all the bulbs you'd like to have. Also mark out where those bulbs should go, on paper or with durable stakes, to avoid confusion when it's time to plant.

Among the delights of High Spring are all the garden tours that take place. Be sure to take along a camera and a notebook to record the things you see that could be added to your garden. This is the perfect way and time to plan future flowers.

opposite: Hyacinth Hybrids Foxglove (*Digitalis purpurea* Hyacinth Hybrids)
Spring Song Strain Columbine (*Aquilegia hybrida* Spring Song Strain)
Showy Deutzia (*Deutzia x magnifica*)
Armand's Clematis (*Clematis armandii*)
Garden Sage (*Salvia officinalis*)
Mountain Bluet (*Centaurea montana*)
Sweet Pea (*Lathyrus odoratus*)
Filipendula (*Filipendula hexapetala*)

The innocent flamboyance of spring flowers brings a cozy excitement to this country-formal dining room. Rising well above the paired Bavarian pitchers, spikes of Hyacinth Hybrids foxgloves are topped with feathery wands of filipendula. Spilling to the left are branches of showy deutzia and star-like blooms of Armand's clematis. Yellow Spring Song Strain columbines, purple spikes of garden sage, and cascading stems of pink sweet peas continue the sweep of color to the right. Tucked into the mouth of each container, mountain bluets emphasize the richness of the grapes on each container.

BELOW: JAPANESE WISTERIA
(*Wisteria floribunda*)

The appearance of wisteria's frosty-
blue, fragrant flowers is one of the
sure signs that spring has truly
sprung. The tangled, cascading form
of these flowers demands to be used
just as they grow. Here, they spill like
grapes from a tall, narrow (and stone-
filled, for balance) blue-and-white
porcelain vase.

LEFT: SALVIA (*Salvia farinacea* Victoria
& Silver White)
COSMOS (*Cosmos bipinnatus* Candy
Stripe)
YARROW (*Achillea millefolium* Cerise
Queen)
DEADNETTLE (*Lamiastrum galeobdolon*
variegatum)

The flower-filled surround of this
arrangement sets both its color
scheme and its botanically intense
conception. The mingled pinks and
whites of Candy Stripe cosmos forms
the central feature; the color of these
flowers is repeated in the clusters of
milfoil pink yarrow. Spikes of blue
Victoria and Silver White salvia lend
an airy outline, as does the grey
foliage of Silver Queen artemisia. The
variegated leaves of trailing deadnettle
complete the feeling of overflow.

RIGHT: PURPLE CONEFLOWER
(*Echinacea purpurea* Bright Star)
CROFTWAY PINK BEE BALM (*Monarda
didyma* Croftway Pink)
LAMB'S EARS (*Stachys lanata*)
SWEET PEA (*Lathyrus odoratus*)
YARROW (*Achillea millefolium* Cerise
Queen)

Pink, grey and green are the
traditional palette of English country
style, which emphasizes casual yet
intricate blends of color, pattern and
texture. Those qualities are captured
here with spidery blooms of Croftway
Pink bee balm, daisy-like purple
coneflowers (which are really pink)
and Cerise Queen yarrow. Fuzzy
spikes of lamb's ear flowers and
trailing stems of sweet pea lend
additional grace and softness.

RIGHT: CAMELOT ROSE (*Rosa* Camelot)
SUNRAY COREOPSIS (*Coreopsis grandiflora* Sunray)
YELLOW TRUMPET HONEYSUCKLE (*Lonicera sempervirens* sulphurea)
CURLY DOCK (*Rumex crispus*)
COMMON RYE (*Secale cereale*)

The rose may be the queen of flowers, but it's an easygoing monarch. Stems of Camelot are here combined with spikes of curly dock, seed heads of common rye and the yellow blooms of Sunray coreopsis and yellow trumpet honeysuckle — all of which are humble, unassuming flowers.

WAKAEBISU AZALEA (*Rhododendron x 'Obtusum'* Wakaebisu)
ENGLISH IVY (*Hedera helix*)
ROSEMARY (*Rosmarinus officinalis*)
WORMWOOD (*Artemisia absinthium*)

The vivid hues of Wakaebisu azalea glow as brightly as the surface of this well-used silver vase. Tendrils of English ivy, sprigs of rosemary and young leaves of wormwood help keep the overall effect soft and casual.

VERNAL IRIS (*Iris verna*)
CHIVES (*Allium schoenoprasum*)
WALLFLOWER (*Cheiranthus cheiri*
Apricot Delight)
DOWNY PHLOX (*Phlox pilosa*)
COMMON SQUILL (*Endymion non-
scriptus* rosea)

When seen up close, small
arrangements lend themselves to
intricate combinations. The clustered,
single blossoms of wild downy phlox,
at left, are balanced with the puff-ball
flowers of chives. Curving spikes of
common squill complete the circular
flow of the composition. Apricot
Delight wallflowers and two small
vernal iris create a glowing,
central focus.

LEFT: FLOWERING DOGWOOD (*Cornus florida*)
DOUBLEFILE VIBURNUM (*Viburnum plicatum* tomentosum)

The classic combination of white and green is universally appealing. Here, white dogwood flowers join with the smaller and more delicate blossoms of doublefile viburnum. Although similar in shape, the clustered viburnum flowers give an extra bit of detail to the combination.

ABOVE: BEST MAN PEONY (*Paeonia* Best Man)
MOON RIVER PEONY (*Paeonia* Moon River)
MOONSTONE PEONY (*Paeonia* Moonstone)
PLUME POPPY (*Macleaya cordata*)
GARDEN SAGE (*Salvia officinalis*)

The opulence of peonies makes them one of the most dramatic and best-loved of springtime flowers. Here, the vivid red of Best Man makes a daring counterpoint to oxblood walls. Pale pink Moon River and white Moonstone add brilliance. The bold, grey-green leaves of plume poppy and spikes of garden sage complete the overall impression of luxurious abundance.

BELOW: RISING SUN IRIS (*Iris kaempferi* Rising Sun)
PLUME POPPY (*Macleaya cordata*)
WORMWOOD (*Artemisia absinthium*)

Grey foliages are the universal medium for brightly colored flowers. The almost tropical appearance of plume poppy and the lacy elegance of wormwood form a silvery surround for the open blooms of Rising Sun iris.

ENGLISH
SUMMER

With the lengthening of days, the garden slowly settles into a more tranquil season. The fresh, bright citron of new foliage deepens to a solid green; the soft pastels of spring give way to richer, deeper hues. Days are sweet and warm, but cool evenings help keep flowers fresh and colors bright. Although we know that hotter weather will be sure to come, it's not upon us yet. These are the garden's halcyon days. This is English Summer.

TAIYO SUNFLOWER (*Helianthus annuus* Taiyo)
PICCOLO SUNFLOWER (*Helianthus annus* Piccolo)
DILL (*Anethum graveolens*)

Gloriously unassuming, the massive heads of Taiyo sunflowers mingle with their smaller cousin, Piccolo. The misty-yellow sprays of dill complete the happy theme of green and gold.

As its name suggests, this season captures all the splendor and abundance of the English flower garden. The British Isles are blessed with temperate climate; winters are mild and summers are moist and gentle. Flowers can be grown in true profusion because the weather lets them last for many weeks.

In North America, however, summers are hot, and even though they are humid, rainfall can be limited. Many flowers simply can't withstand the stress. Even so, we do have a few weeks of glorious, gentle weather before the heat becomes intense. During that brief time, our gardens capture and compress the entire British summer into a month or so.

Perennials are the hallmark of the English Summer garden. Phlox, lilies, yarrow, coreopsis, salvias, black-eyed Susans, daylilies, gooseneck, Veronica hollyhocks, Japanese iris, shasta daisies, monarda and lythrum flourish in this season. These plants will frequently continue to flower on and off from now until frost but never again with the vigor and profusion of this first explosion that warm weather brings.

Most perennials, of course, take several years to reach maturity. They need some time to get established before they have the energy and size to really make a show. Thus, the potential of this season is too often overlooked by gardeners. It does take planning, but when the plants begin to bloom, our time, effort and patience are rewarded, and the flowers of this season seem all the more delightful because they are hard-won. It is also true that once established most perennials live for years, so a little investment now is more than compensated by the prospects of the future.

Flowering shrubs are also part of the English Summer's palette—abelia, buddlia, vitex, Saint Johnswort, deciduous azaleas, roses and hydrangeas, to name just a few. Aside from flowers, these plants increase the scale of plantings in the garden. They also lend a necessary balance and solidity.

Although there are a few essential chores to be performed, English Summer is really an easy season. Our chief concerns are making preparations for the coming of hot weather. A good, thick layer of mulch, for example, will help insulate the soil against heat and will help conserve moisture in the ground. It also helps reduce the amount of weeding required. We can also plan and plant our annuals for later season color. Most garden centers will have good stocks of bedding plants and seeds available; the pleasant weather makes it easy to give a little extra care to their planting. Till in generous amounts of compost, peat and sand as you set plants — along with a time-released plant food — to get annuals off to a good start.

For the most part, English Summer is a time to sit back and enjoy. It really is one of the few times in the year that we can truly live in the garden. Temperatures are very comfortable, and bugs aren't yet a problem. Outdoor dining is one of the great joys of English Summer. Entertaining in the garden is the perfect way to share this special season with family and friends.

RIGHT: MIXED LILIES (*Lilium* White Flower Farm Naturalizing, Pastel Mix)
BUTTERFLY WEED (*Asclepias tuberosa*)
OAKLEAF HYDRANGEA (*Hydrangea quercifolia*)
GOLD PLATE YARROW (*Achillea filipendulina* Gold Plate)
SUNBURST COREOPSIS (*Coreopsis grandiflora* Sunburst)
GARDEN SAGE (*Salvia officinalis*)

The massiveness of this arrangement is lightened by the flower colors, the pickled basket and the airy stems of Johnson grass. A crock inside the basket was first filled with branches of oakleaf hydrangea blooms and the foliage of garden sage. Next, bright orange butterfly weed was laid over the basket's edge; this network of stems then made it possible to add the upright stems of lilies, Gold Plate yarrow and Sunburst coreopsis.

LEFT: BLACK-EYED SUSANS (*Rudbeckia serotina*)
MEADOW FESCUE (*Festuca elatior*)
FOOL'S PARSLEY (*Aethusa cynapium*)

The abundance of a country roadside was gathered up to fill this antique copper measure. The height of this container lets the flowers be used untrimmed, mimicking in miniature their natural appearance in the landscape. Black-eyed Susans, fool's parsley and the seedheads of meadow fescue prove the foolishness of labeling non-garden flowers "weeds."

LEFT: MEDALLION ROSE (*Rosa*
Medallion)
BRANDY ROSE (*Rosa x* Brandy)
WHITE LIGHTNING ROSE (*Rosa* White
Lightning)
LADY ROSE (*Rosa* Lady)
SHEER BLISS ROSE (*Rosa* Sheer Bliss)
CHINESE ELM (*Ulmus parvifolia*)

The soft, glowing colors of five soft
pastel roses — Medallion, Brandy,
White Lightning, Lady and Sheer
Bliss — and the rose-like foliage of
Chinese elm need nothing else,
except to be enjoyed.

CALLA LILY (*Zantedeschia aethiopica*)
ICICLE VERONICA (*Veronica longifolia* Icicle)
GOOSENECK LOOSESTRIFE (*Lysimachia clethroides*)
SILVER QUEEN ARTEMISIA (*Artemisia ludoviciana* Silver Queen)

Calla lilies may be elegant, but they are often self-conscious beauties. These garden-grown specimens, however, have a pure simplicity that's free of affectation. Mixed with curving spikes of Icicle veronica and gooseneck loosestrife, these white flowers are set off by the lacy grey foliage of Silver Queen artemisia. The foliage of gooseneck adds a handsome texture.

RIGHT: FRENCH HYDRANGEA (*Hydrangea macrophylla*)
SWEET PEA (*Lathyrus odoratus*)
PLUME POPPY (*Macleaya cordata*)

The luxuriant foliage of hydrangea makes a perfect foil for its varicolored flowers. A trailing branch of sweet peas and the feathery blooms of plume poppy provide a necessary change of pace from the hydrangea's boldness.

LEFT: Regale Lily (*Lilium* Regale)
Green Magic Lily (*Lilium* Green
Magic)
Golden Splendor Lily (*Lilium*
Golden Splendor)
Yellow Tiger Lily (*Lilium* Yellow
Tiger)
Plume Poppy (*Macleaya cordata*)
Victoria Salvia (*Salvia farinacea*
Victoria)
Gooseneck Loosestrife (*Lysimachia
clethroides*)
Greenbriar Smilax (*Smilax
rotundifolia*)

The mingling of several types of lilies
gives a luxurious effect without
completely denuding the garden.
Here, four types of these fragrant
flowers — Regale, Green Magic,
Golden Splendor and Yellow Tiger —
were chosen for their easy mix of
colors. The boldness of these blooms
is tempered by the airy stems of
plume poppy, gooseneck loosestrife
and the flowers and foliage of
greenbriar smilax. Spikes of Victoria
salvia were also tucked into the
composition to pick out the dark blue
in the floral paper.

RIGHT: WILD SWEET WILLIAM (*Phlox maculata* Alpha)
FRENCH HYDRANGEA (*Hydrangea macrophylla*)
MORDEN'S PINK LYTHRUM (*Lythrum salicaria* Morden's Pink)
PURPLE JAPANESE MAPLE (*Acer palmatum* atropurpureum)
LADYBELLS (*Adenophora confusa*)

Although the body of this arrangement is quite dense, spikey flowers and foliages help keep it from appearing "stuffed." The glowing pink of wild sweet William is framed with pale, lavender-pink heads of French hydrangea. Spires of ladybells, arching stems of Morden's Pink lythrum and dark purple, star-like leaves of Japanese maple break free of the central, compact mass.

DEEP SUMMER

PREVIOUS PAGE: BRIGHT LIGHTS
COSMOS (*Cosmos sulphureus* Bright
Lights)

A glass container filled with Bright
Lights cosmos makes a dramatic
accent for this elegant tray of
afternoon "essentials."

here simply is no use pretending that Deep Summer will be anything but hot and long. Once the jet stream starts to pump that sultry, humid air up from the tropics, we're in for a bout of discomfort. The garden doesn't have to suffer, however. If we provide sufficient water, summer can be flower-filled.

Not every Deep Summer day, of course, is unrelentingly oppressive. Even in the middle of the summer, we are sometimes treated to delightful respites of low humidity and temperatures. The trick for gardening is to arrange our schedules so that we can take advantage of the opportunities these days present and of mornings and evenings, which tend to be quite pleasant.

Annuals are a natural choice for summer gardens. Most of them are native to the tropics and subtropics, so they are ideally suited to this season. They thrive in temperatures that make us wilt. Once they are established, they are easy to maintain, demanding little more than a good, long drink of water. Also, annuals tend to be fast growing, so even if they do begin to lag in summer's heat, we can simply rip them out and plant another batch of seeds. They're inexpensive, so we can afford to plant them in abundance. Best of all, most annuals will actually benefit from cutting so that the more we gather, the more flowers they produce. We can freely cut vast quantities of flowers from our summer gardens to enjoy indoors.

Deep Summer flowers aren't, however, limited to annuals alone. Perennials like daylilies, rudbeckias, echinacea, phlox, lythrum, dahlias and true lilies also lend their beauty to the summer garden. And there are several types of shrubs with summer flowers: hydrangeas, roses, buddleia, abelia, nandina, vitex, Anthony Waterer spiraea, pittisporum and gardenia. Besides the flowers, we should not forget to enjoy, in both the garden and indoors, the beauty of plants themselves. Hostas, coleus, artemisia, caladiums, ferns, fennel and dill are especially valued for their handsome foliages.

Another way we can enjoy the summer garden is to plant it with those kinds of flowers that best suit the time of day that we're outdoors. Many summer flowers are sweetly scented—nicotiana, gingerlily, true lilies, certain hostas, phlox and, of course, roses. Since the fragrance of these flowers tends to be intensified by cooler, moister air, they're perfect for a place near the terrace so that we can enjoy their perfume when we come out-of-doors in the evening's cool.

SONYA ROSE (*Rosa* Sonya)
CANDIDUM CALADIUM (*Caladium bicolor* Candidum)
FRAGRANT HOSTA (*Hosta plantaginea* grandiflora)
FORTUNE'S HOSTA (*Hosta fortunei* albomarginiata)
SMALL-LEAVED HOSTA (*Hosta tardiflora*)
VARIEGATED LIRIOPE (*Liriope muscari* variegata)
VARIEGATED AUCUBA (*Aucuba japonica* variegata)
NANDINA (*Nandina domestica*)
HAY-SCENTED FERN (*Dennstaedtia punctilobula*)

A single rose can be enough to make a whole arrangement. The slightly overblown Sonya blossom forms the focal point of a rich mix of green and variegated foliages: Candidum caladium, the upright leaves of fragrant hosta and variegated liriope, variegated aucuba, ridged small-leaved hosta, sprigs of nandina foliage and a spray of variegated hosta leaves.

RUFFLES HYBRIDS ZINNIAS (*Zinnia elegans* Ruffles Hybrids)
DAHLIA FLOWERED MIXED ZINNIAS (*Zinnia elegans* Dahlia Flowered Mixed)

Zinnias are typically regarded as old-fashioned, country flowers. This mix of Ruffles and Dahlia Flowered Mixed selections, however, is anything but plain and ordinary. To get a loose effect, half the flowers were gathered up and dropped into place; additional stems were then added to create a non-symmetrical mass. The white zinnias were added last to evenly distribute this accent color throughout the richly hued collage from a Deep Summer garden.

We can also plant flowers that work, physically and psychologically, with summer. Although we tend to think of summer flowers in terms of vivid, hot, bright colors, they also come in soft pastels and white. Lighter colors make us feel cooler because they don't directly remind us of the intensity of the sun. Equally important, white or pastel flowers will reflect more light, so we'll especially appreciate them at night. In the garden after the sun begins to set, these flowers will stand out from the shadows. We can enjoy both our flowers and our comfort in the garden.

Watering is by far the most important summer garden chore. And like all other aspects of living with this season, it is a job that's better done when it is cool — early in the morning or in the evening. Watering when it's cool helps reduce evaporation; it also gives plants water when their metabolisms are best able to absorb it. Long, deep waterings, even if they have to be done on a rationed basis, are always better than frequent sprinklings. Otherwise, the water stays near the surface of the soil.

Deadheading, or removing faded blooms, is another necessary task. If allowed to go to seed, most plants, and especially annuals, will tend to stop setting flower buds, and that cuts short their length of bloom. Remove just the faded flowers, however, to avoid damage to developing buds.

Deep Summer tests the stamina of both the garden and the gardener. But with a little extra effort, the summer garden can be a true delight. This is, after all, the longest season; since days are also longer, we're given ample time to enjoy its beauty.

SUNFLOWERS (*Helianthus annuus* mixed)

The varied shapes and sizes of mixed sunflowers make a spritely, tongue-in-cheek juxtaposition to this elegant, urbane environment.

RIGHT: PEEGEE HYDRANGEA
(*Hydrangea paniculata* grandiflora)
PLUME POPPY (*Macleaya cordata*)
BELLS OF IRELAND (*Moluccella laevis*)

A gathering of pottery jugs is
complemented by the bold, massive
flowers of peegee hydrangeas. The
green flowers of bells of Ireland subtly
pick up the green, unopened flowers
of the hydrangeas, while spikes of
plume poppy flowers lend a soft, airy
counterpoint to the otherwise heavy
composition.

DOMINO HYBRIDS NICOTIANA
(*Nicotiana alata* Domino Hybrids)
MORNING MIST MADAGASCAR
PERIWINKLE (*Vinca rosea*
Morning Mist)
PINK QUEEN SPIDER FLOWER (*Cleome spinosa* Pink Queen)
HELEN CAMPBELL SPIDER FLOWER
(*Cleome spinosa* Helen Campbell)

Towards the end of summer, garden flowers tend to become a bit lanky; a good cutting back is in order. But the easy, flowing nature of those trimmings can be splendid in arrangements. Long, arching stems of Domino Hybrids nicotiana, Morning Mist madagascar periwinkle and pink and white cleome were gathered up, dropped into the vase and simply allowed to "flop" in an unassuming way.

LEFT: SWEET CONEFLOWERS
(*Rudbeckia subtomentosa*)
RUSTIC COLORS CONEFLOWERS
(*Rudbeckia hirta* Rustic Colors)
ARMAND'S CLEMATIS (*Clematis
armandii*)

Sweet coneflowers, gathered from the
roadside, are mixed with their fancy
cousins, Rustic Colors, a hybrid black-
eyed Susan. The play of names,
backgrounds and characters of these
flowers is like the setting: a happy mix
of old and new. The large strap foliage
of Armand's clematis resembles the
coarse-textured leaves of the
coneflowers.

FRENCH HYDRANGEA (*Hydrangea macrophylla*)
PRIME MINISTER PHLOX (*Phlox paniculata* Prime Minister)
WAVY-LEAVED HOSTA (*Hosta undulata*)
SOUTHERN SHIELD FERN (*Thelypteris kunthii*)
MARIE'S VARIEGATED FRENCH HYDRANGEA (*Hydrangea macrophylla* Variegated Mariesii)

Fresh pastels, green and white, are summer mainstays. Here, several shades of French hydrangea and the white-edged foliage of Marie's variegated hydrangea set the body of the composition. Fronds of southern shield fern, hosta flowers and white Prime Minister phlox are all sweetly scented — an especially delightful comfort on a humid summer day.

RIGHT: Snow-on-the-Mountain
(*Euphorbia bicolor*)
Rue (*Ruta graveolens*)
Virgin's Bower Clematis (*Clematis virginiana*)
Royal Standard Hosta (*Hosta* Royal Standard)

The refreshing mix of white and green takes on a bit of drama when it's placed in a coolly-classical situation. Branches of variegated snow-on-the-mountain, blue-green rue foliage, and tendrils of virgin's bower clematis provide the base and structure of the arrangement. Tall, fragrant flowers of Royal Standard hosta lend an airy loftiness to the fullness of the central mass.

LEFT: BUTTERFLY LILY
(*Hedychium coronarium*)
AFFINIS NICOTIANA (*Nicotiana affinis*)
WHITE CLOUD BUDDLEIA (*Buddleia davidii* White Cloud)

The perfume of fragrant flowers is intensified when they are placed in smallish spaces, like this bath. The exotic foliage and flowers of butterfly lily, star-like blooms of Affinis nicotiana and White Cloud buddleia spires were chosen for their harmony of color, texture and scent.

ABOVE: MONTEBRETIA
(*Crocosmia x crocosmiiflora*)
BRONZE FENNEL (*Foeniculum vulgare*
Baloquese)

Bronze fennel flowers and montbretia
(crocosmia blooms and foliage mix
dramatically with crisp-edged,
contemporary furnishings. The glass
cylinder suits the modernist tome of
"less is more" by incorporating the
stems of the flowers into the
composition.

AUTUMN

The brilliant foliages of Autumn permit a lavish, large-scaled celebration of the season. Here, the glowing leaves of sugar maple and the deeper, russet hues of oakleaf hydrangea foliage capture the intensity and sheer delight of autumn's amber light.

Autumn reinvigorates the gardener and the garden. After the weight of summer's heat and dog-day afternoons, the first cool days of fall bring us back to life. Lower temperatures help revive our summer-weary gardens, too. Annuals and roses both will tend to set new buds with the return of cooler days. Throughout the garden, new growth gives way to maturity.

Fall is, of course, the time for "color." We look with expectation for those bright spots of red, orange, rust and yellow in the tops of trees. We also watch for that delicious honey-gold of autumn light. Morning, noon and evening, it suffuses everything beneath it with a gentle, amber glow. And the sky becomes azure. Almost always clear, the crisp, blue air and golden light of autumn slowly dissolve into the purple night.

Autumn color also comes with flowers — goldenrod, coneflowers, dahlias, Japanese anemonies, Michaelmas daisies, wild asters, chrysanthemums, knotweed, Mexican sage, wild ageratum and sedum. These fall blooming plants seem to have been designed with autumn's light and sky in mind. Some, like goldenrod, coneflowers and many types of mums, capture the golden glory of the sun, while others, such as asters, sage and ageratum, are like distillations of the sky and misty shadows of autumn's afternoons. Together, these flowers celebrate the harmony of this season of fulfillment.

As the time of harvest, autumn is in many ways a natural conclusion to the year. At the same time, it is a time of promise and thanksgiving. In the garden, there has not been such abundance since spring. Unlike springtime's pastel cloud, however, autumn envelops us with crystalline delights. Color pours down from the trees and spreads across the ground in brilliant jewel tones. From the liquid amber of the sweetgum trees to the garnet red of sumac, everything about autumn is sharply focused and intense and stirs excitement. As we look for ways to express our energy, the garden is there, waiting for our attention.

Autumn offers certain gardening benefits which spring cannot afford. First, there is the matter of time.

RIGHT: BITTERNUT HICKORY (*Carya cordiformis*)
CHESTNUT OAK (*Quercus prinus*)
YELLOW-BERRIED NANDINA (*Nandina domestica* lutea)
NANDINA (*Nandina domestica*)
LOLLIPOP BLANKET FLOWER (*Gaillardia pulchella* Lollipop)
GAIETY BLANKET FLOWER (*Gaillardia pulchella* Gaiety)
JOHNSON GRASS (*Sorgum halepense*)

The sparkle of gold and brass highlights the glowing richness of this autumn gathering. Bitternut hickory leaves establish a flowing background for a centrally placed rosette of green and yellow chestnut oak leaves. A cascade of grape-like yellow nandina berries and sprays of Lollipop blanket flowers complete the outline. Red nandina berries, yellow Gaiety blanket flower and sprigs of Johnson grass are final accents.

Autumn days are long and gentle and the pace less hectic. Because it simply isn't possible to do, with any satisfaction, everything that can be done in spring, many chores were done in haste while others simply had to be left incomplete. If we take advantage of the fall, we can not only catch up but really get ahead of things.

Besides benefits to the gardener, there are dividends for plants, too, that get their start in autumn. Since roots continue to grow well into the winter and root growth normally resumes long before foliage or flowers appear in spring, autumn-planted trees and shrubs have a definite advantage over those planted in spring. They grow faster, and their well-developed roots make them better able to withstand summer droughts.

Another benefit of autumn planting is climate. Unlike capricious spring, which freely mixes rain and sun with intermittent thaws and frosts, the autumn is more temperate and predictable. Gardening activities are less susceptible to interruption by sporadic rains, and since the ground is dry, soils can be worked with greater ease.

Further, autumn plants can be a bargain. In spring, when everyone has garden fever, the demand for plants keeps prices high. But as winter approaches, many nurseries and garden centers are anxious to reduce their stocks to simplify their wintering procedures. They've tended plants in top condition all year long. Now they're ready to conclude their business, so in autumn we may find larger plants at lower costs.

As days grow shorter and colder, we, too, begin to think about concluding our garden business. Leaves must be raked and placed on the compost pile; mulches must be set in place against the coming winter. We tuck our gardens to bed and leave them to their winter's rest.

OPPOSITE: BLACK-EYED SUSANS (*Rudbeckia hirta*)
EARLY GOLDENROD (*Solidago juncea*)
ENGLISH IVY (*Hedera helix*)
TAIYO SUNFLOWER (*Helianthus annuus* Taiyo)
RYE GRASS (*Secale cereale*)

Gathered from the edges of a meadow, wildflowers prove the beauty of nature's richness. Black-eyed Susans, early goldenrod and rye grass seed heads are the sure signs of the start of fall. Tendrils of English ivy and a single Taiyo sunflower from the garden add grace and boldness.

BELOW: KNOTWEED
(*Polygonum lapathifolium*)
JOHNSON GRASS (*Sorghum halepense*)
WILD ASTER (*Aster azureus*)
AUTUMN GAY-FEATHER (*Liatris squarrosa*)

The beauty of autumn fills the landscape abundantly. Even "weeds" from a fallow field provide a welcome gathering of color. The vivid pink, pearl-like blooms of wild knotweed, echoed by the bronzy seed heads of Johnson grass, were simply stuffed into place. Wild aster and autumn gay-feather each provide a note of frosty lavender.

RIGHT: TARTARIAN ASTERS
(*Aster tartaricus*)
WILD AGERATUM (*Eupatorium coelestinum*)
MEXICAN SAGE (*Salvia leucantha*)

Lavenders and silver make a gleaming combination. The body of this composition is supplied by branches of Tartarian asters. Wild geranium and spikes of Mexican sage intensify the frosty colors and daisy-like shapes of the asters.

WASHINGTON HAWTHORN (*Crataegus phaenopyrum*)
CAROLINA SNAILSEED (*Cocculus carolinus*)

The shapely branches and clustered berries of Washington hawthorn are used here, as in nature, as a splendid sculptural tangle. The brilliant red, translucent berries and frosty, marbled foliage of Carolina snailseed spill down one side of the container.

CITIES OF DESTINY

THE ART OF NEW YORK

AMERICAN BEECH (*Fagus grandifolia*)
PERSIMMON (*Diospyros virginiana*)
CHRYSANTHEMUMS
(*Chrysanthemum spp.*)
BRACKEN FERN (*Pteridium aquilinum*)
JOHNSON GRASS (*Sorghum halepense*)

The classical appearance of this arrangement grows from both its setting and the nature of its elements. Secured with a metal frog, branches of the papery beech leaves set the background and the outline of the composition. Next, branches of wild persimmon foliage and fruit were set at angles to create a network of interlocking stems. One by one, twelve different types of garden mums were then used to create the central mass. Finally, dried fronds of bracken fern and tall seed heads of Johnson grass were added for airy fullness.

LEFT: PEEGEE HYDRANGEA
(*Hydrangea paniculata* grandiflora)
GOLDSTURM CONEFLOWER (*Rudbeckia fulgida* Goldsturm)
LATE GOLDENROD (*Solidago gigantea*)
SENSATION COSMOS (*Cosmos bipinnatus* Sensation Mixed)

The lavishness of the floral paper and fabric in this room just seemed to call for an equally baroque arrangement. Beginning with stems of peegee hydrangeas, which are slightly flushed with pink, the basket was then filled with coneflowers and later goldenrod. Bright pink and magenta Sensation cosmos pick out the background colors.

RIGHT: SUTTER'S GOLD ROSE
(*Rosa x* Sutter's Gold)
SHERWOOD PEACH DAHLIAS (*Dahlia x* Sherwood Peach)
DWARF DOUBLE PINCUSHION FLOWER (*Scabiosa atropurpurea* Dwarf Double Mixed)
ALBA JAPANESE ANEMONIES (*Anemone hupehensis* alba)
ROSE GERANIUM (*Pelargonium graveolens*)

Many times, the color harmonies of an arrangement grow directly from the richness of a single flower. The glowing pink with yellow highlights of a Sutter's Gold rose inspired the choice of Sherwood Peach dahlias. Although their color closely matches that of the rose, a closer look reveals a pale wash of lavender along the dahlia's outer petals. This color is repeated, more intensely, in Dwarf Double pincushion flowers. A few white forms of these flowers are matched with Japanese anemonies. The yellow stamens of these later flowers, which pick up the undertones of both the roses and dahlias, are effective even on stems that have lost their petals. The frosted green of rose geranium foliage adds a play of name and texture.

ABOVE: STERLING SILVER DAHLIA
(*Dahlia* Sterling Silver)
PURE WHITE NICOTIANA (*Nicotiana
alata* Pure White)
JAPANESE ANEMONE (*Anemone hupehensis*
alba)
CANADA GOLDENROD (*Solidago
canadensis*)

The weight of dahlia flowers
frequently results in twisted, arching
stems. Taking advantage of this
characteristic, several branches of
Sterling Silver dahlias were first set
into place, along with sprigs of Pure
White nicotiana. White Japanese
anemonies and fluffy heads of Canada
goldenrod were then tucked in to
soften the boldness of the dahlias.

RIGHT: BONESET
(*Eupatorium perfoliatum*)
ALMA POTSCHKE ASTER (*Aster novae-
angliae* Alma Potschke)
HARRINGTON'S PINK ASTER (*Aster
novae-angliae* Harrington's Pink)
SILVERLACE VINE (*Polygonum aubertii*)
GARDEN SAGE (*Salvia officinalis*)

The silvers, greys and dusky pinks of
autumn afternoons are echoed in the
flowers of this season. Here, two types
of asters — rosy-lavender Alma
Potschke and Harrington's Pink — are
set between a hazy cloud of boneset,
left, and a cascade of silverlace vine
blooms. The strap-like leaves of
garden sage provide a handsome
contrast to the filigree of flowers.

BELOW: BRANDY ROSE (*Rosa x* Brandy)
PEACE ROSE (*Rosa x* Peace)
CLIMBING PIÑATA ROSE (*Rosa x*
Climbing Piñata)
AMERICA BEECH (*Fagus grandifolia*)
NANDINA (*Nandina domestica*)
WILD ROSE (*Rosa virginiana*)

The last of Autumn's roses, gathered
just before the first hard frost, display
the mottled coloring produced by
growing cold. Brandy, Peace and gold-
and-red Climbing Piñata blooms take
on poignant élegance against the
richly patterned leaves of American
beech. At left, nandina berries and a
few sprigs of wild rose hips intensify
the reds within the garden roses.

WINTER

RIGHT: Nandina (*Nandina domestica*)
Yaupon Holly (*Ilex vomitoria*)
Staghorn Sumac (*Rhus typhina*)
Chinese Tallow Tree (*Sapium
sebiferum*)
Tabasco Pepper (*Capsicum frutescens*)
Burford Holly (*Ilex cornuta*
Burfordii)
Althaea (*Hibiscus syriacus*)

Greenery and berries are the hallmarks of the winter holidays. They are also mainstays of the winter garden. Here, they form the perfect focus for a winter luncheon shared with fellow gardeners. Arranged in a long, narrow basket, the centerpiece is low enough to still permit across-the-table conversation. Sprigs of Burford holly leaves and berries form the base of the arrangement; they also help conceal the metal liner that holds water. Next, stems of red nandina berries, yaupon holly and the cone-like pods of sumac were inserted through the holly base to give a bit of height and fullness. The hard, white fruits of Chinese tallow tree (sometimes known as popcorn tree) and fiery-red tabasco peppers were then added to create a central focus. Finally, a few brown pods of althaea were added to repeat the color and the texture of the basket.

 s the wind turns from the north, it whispers in the treetops, "frost." Although the day was bright and warm, the shadows of the afternoon are tinged with lavender and chill. The night arrives without a pause for twilight; as it deepens, a silver dust is scattered on the ground. And in the pale grey light of morning, the sparkle on each blade of grass announces Winter's advent.

There is a special beauty to be found in winter gardens. Distilled to simple outlines, shapes and volumes, the garden is truly revealed as a work of sculpture. There are few bright colors to distract our

eyes. Everything is seen in sharp detail. The boldness of the evergreens, the calligraphy of branches and the contrast of light and shade are never so clearly seen as in this unassuming season.

Not everyone, however, is willing to see the charms of leafless plants. We're prejudiced by that "dead-of-winter" syndrome. Deciduous plants aren't "dead" in winter, of course, as the ageless cycle of the seasons clearly proves. They merely shed what has become unnecessary foliage. By dropping their leaves, deciduous plants concentrate their energy on root growth and on their developing buds, which are the source of flowers later in the year.

But it would be naive to ignore the problems that come with deciduous plants. They *can* appear forlorn. And yet, this is rarely the fault of plants. It's more a problem of faulty planting on our parts.

Because they are essentially transparent, leafless deciduous plants require a background to display their patterns and subtle colorings. They need a wall, fence, hedge or an expanse of grass to set off their shapes and outlines. These backgrounds must, of course, reinforce the garden's total plan.

Large-growing evergreens like hollies, Southern magnolia, spruce, fir and hemlock make dramatic garden backgrounds. Their height and density establish privacy along the garden's borders; their rich green color

LEFT: AMERICAN BEECH (*Fagus grandifolia*)
POSSUM HAW (*Ilex decidua*)
RED MAPLE (*Acer rubrum*)
OAKLEAF HYDRANGEA (*Hydrangea quercifolia*)
SMOOTH ALDER (*Alnus rugosa*)
BROOM-SEDGE (*Andropogon virginicus*)

This arrangement celebrates the "weeds" of agriculture — native plants that thrive without the need of cultivation. Gathered from the meadows and the hedgerows of a farm, the mix of berries, foliages and stalwart winter flowers seems ideally suited to this simple farmhouse room. It also offers the advantage of longevity. None of these materials requires a source of water. The foliages and the hydrangea flowers had dried naturally; the berries and the maple and alder flowers will retain their shape and color as they slowly dry indoors. Stems were simply wedged between the straps of the oak basket and into the holes of three construction bricks, which also serve to keep the basket steady. The upright, berried branches of possum haw were tucked in first, along with several stems of alder with its tassled, yellow flowers. Horizontal branches of beech leaves were then inserted, sideways, to extend the mass beyond the basket. Arching stems of parchment-like oakleaf hydrangea flowers were also used to reinforce this outward movement. This extended space is repeated, on the left, by several twisted stems of maple, which have tiny red and yellow flowers at their tips. Finally, the golden plumes of broom-sedge were inserted to add fullness at the center.

also makes a necessary counterpoint to winter's predominance of greys and browns. And when they are used in concert with deciduous plants, evergreens become both accent and supporting counterpart.

Although winter is basically a time when the garden is at rest, growth continues deep within the ground. Roots are only dormant when the ground is frozen hard. Life also continues in the stems and buds of plants, so a few gardening chores are called for in winter.

Since water is their source of life, plants may require a winter watering. Sharp winds can dehydrate both evergreens and deciduous plants. If the winter has been especially dry, dehydration can become a serious problem. Winter irrigation is, therefore, one of this season's chief concerns. Deep waterings during those occasional mild days can make a tremendous difference in the way plants weather winter's sometimes harsher side.

Mulches are also important for plants to survive the winter. They protect shallow-rooted plants from frost heave; they conserve soil moisture. They also help keep plants from sprouting prematurely by insulating soil and keeping it at an even temperature.

Reduced to simple armatures of branch, twig and stem, deciduous plants in winter reveal the grace of nature unadorned. Admittedly, this is a subtle charm; compared to flowers and foliages, it may seem incidental. But where, at present, is there basis for comparison? The northwest winds have swept away all trace of leaf and bloom. And that which had been hidden is now manifest and magnified.

It does, however, take a certain generosity—a sympathy of vision and a willingness of heart—to see the leafless plants of winter and to find them lovely. But if we make the effort, there are wonders to behold.

SOUTHERN MAGNOLIA (*Magnolia grandiflora*)
LEATHERLEAF MAHONIA (*Mahonia bealei*)
CHINABERRY (*Melia azedarach*)
VARIEGATED AUCUBA (*Aucuba japonica variegata*)
WHITE PINE (*Pinus strobus*)
FRUITLAND ELAEAGNUS (*Elaeagnus pungens* Fruitland)
JAPANESE ANISE (*Illicum anisatum*)
FLORIDA LEUCOTHOE (*Leucothoe populifolia*)
LUSTERLEAF HOLLY (*Ilex latifolia*)

Dead of Winter? Perish the thought. This lively mix of evergreens proclaims the true vitality of that season. Constructed from the bottom up, the arrangement started with stems of variegated aucuba and Southern magnolia inserted into a short, fat crock that's hidden inside an English market basket. Arching stems of Florida leucothoe and holly-like leatherleaf mahonia were added next for additional fullness and height. Stems of Japanese anise and lusterleaf holly—both of which resemble the dark, glossy leaves of magnolia—were then inserted to complete the outline. Wiry, upright branches of Fruitland elaeagnus and the graceful, feathery stems of white pine were also added to give extra height and contrast to the massiveness of other foliages.

Finally, the leafless stems of Chinaberry branches were tucked in to emphasize the yellow of the aucuba foilage and the background color of the walls. Massive, yet graceful, this arrangement captures both the boldness and the eloquence that is the winter garden.

LEFT: SWEET OLIVE (*Osmanthus fragrans*)
SILVER-EDGED THYME (*Thymus serpyllum* albo-marginata)
COMMON THYME (*Thymus vulgaris*)
SWEET WOODRUFF (*Asperula odorata*)
GERMANDER (*Teucrium chamaedrys*)

Despite their unassuming size, the flowers of sweet olive are intensely fragrant. A single plant can fill a garden with perfume. And since their scent is amplified by warmth, it only takes a sprig or two to fill a room with heady promises of spring. Here, the creamy flowers are framed with their own foliage and with sprigs of aromatic herbs—silver and common thyme, sweet woodruff and germander.

INDEX